A Spiritual Awakening

Poetic Inspiration for The Soul

A Spiritual Awakening

Poetic Inspiration for The Soul

Evangelist Keisha D. Haynes

Copyright

Copyright © 2020 Keisha D. Haynes. All rights reserved. This book or any portion thereof may not be reproduced or used in any manner whatsoever without the express written permission of the publisher and author except for the use of brief quotations in a book review.

Unless otherwise noted, scriptures marked KJV are taken from the KING JAMES VERSION (KJV): KING JAMES VERSION and are public domain.

"Scripture quotations are taken from the Amplified® Bible (AMP), Copyright © 2015 by The Lockman Foundation Used by permission. www.Lockman.org"

"Scripture taken from the New King James Version®. Copyright © 1982 by Thomas Nelson, Inc. Used by permission. All rights reserved."

Printed in the United States of America

First Printing, 2020

ISBN: 978-1-951883-25-6

The Butterfly Typeface Publishing

PO Box 56193

Little Rock AR 72215

www.thebutterflytypeface.com

Honorably Dedicated

To my beautiful, belated mother, Sylvia Marie Johnson, who passed away from a drug overdose on April 12, 2016:

Mom, without you, there would be no me. I dedicate this book to you because your life was not in vain and your pain was for a purpose. Your fight to live despite your struggle inspired me to advocate wholeheartedly healing, wholeness, and freedom to many others. I am truly grateful that you loved me to the best of your ability, and I am truly indebted to you for the prayers you prayed for me. Through me, your legacy will live on to awaken the souls that are plagued with bondages, addictions, and infirmities that have robbed people from the joys of life.

To my belated Grandmother, Rosemary Robertson, who passed away from kidney failure, on November 19, 2009:

Grandma, my last words to you were, "Where is your faith?" I only knew to say that because that is what you instilled in me. I dedicate this book to you because you introduced me to Christ at a very young age, and taught me how to serve. You raised me to be a woman of God, and you ensured that I was grounded in Church every Sunday, Sunday school, choir, usher board, and much more. That is how I know Proverbs 22:6 to be true, "Train up a child in the way he should go: and when he is old, he will not depart from it." You put plenty hours into *training me up*, and because that foundation of faith was laid, I am the woman I am today. Grandma, I am truly grateful for your selflessness, your love, and the compassion you shared with me. You truly were my rock. Thank you for always believing in me.

To my belated mother in law, Evelyn Haynes, who passed away from lung cancer on January 5, 2019:

Mimi, you've always called me your daughter in love, and I thank you for accepting me with your whole heart. I thank you for encouraging me to gain a personal relationship with Christ. You inspired me to learn of Jesus Christ as my savior in a more intimate way. You influenced me to dig deeper and get to know God for myself, learning His will, His way, and His statutes. Your profound wisdom of the word of God motivated me to read God's word more proficiently. Thank you, because of you, I learned to listen to God's still voice. I learned to walk by faith even the more and most importantly, I learned Proverbs 3:5, "Trust in the LORD with all your heart, and do not lean on your own understanding." Thank you for all that you poured into me; your prayers and labor was not in vain.

"You shall love the LORD your God with all your heart and with all your soul and with all your might."

Deuteronomy 6:5

Table of Contents

Introduction 19

Born into Brokenness 25

Sold Out to Christ 33

God Is Trying to Tell You Something 43

Restoration 53

Purification 65

Faith Your Miracle 77

The Sacrificial Life 87

The Worship Experience 97

Redemption 107

Created to Birth 117

The Transfiguration 127

Purpose Driven 137

Conclusion 147

About the Author 149

Foreword

Keisha D. Haynes is the epitome of a woman who has faced and endured many levels of opposition, heartache, disappointment, rejection, pain, and abandonment. She decided to take all that was working against her by the horns and turn what should have kept her broken and wounded into lessons of wisdom, triumph, overcoming, and most of all victory!

Due to her parents being broken and unable to raise her properly, Haynes was raised by her grandmother, who strived to create a home environment that gave her love. Keisha was placed on a path of broken promises, hurt, pain, anger, all while living in a home full of love.

Keisha understood that love helped fill voids of emptiness. She also realized there was more that needed to take place in her life to experience peace and wholeness. She realized that she needed to be healed in her soul.

With much prayer and seeking the face of God, Keisha heard instruction from the Lord and began to write. As she wrote what she heard, her writings turned into poetry, which then turned into poetic words of healing. The more she wrote, the more she began to see that the words written were bottled up feelings and emotions that could not be articulated verbally. The words were an expression of her wounded soul.

Keisha wrote her way into healing for her soul. As you begin to read the words of every poetic piece written in this book, I challenge you to allow these same words that heal the very soul of the author, to break the silence of your soul that will bring about such healing that you will experience forgiveness, peace, and soul prosperity as the Bible tells us in 3 John 1:2. May the contents of the book bring about an awakening that will provoke an everlasting change in your mind, heart, and soul.

Danielle Nicole

Acknowledgments

I've been blessed to have many people who've supported me on my Spiritual Awakening Journey. First and foremost, my husband, Walter Ryan, who is an amazing helpmate. I am so grateful that God has blessed me with Ryan, he is always supporting, believing, encouraging, and investing in me. Growing up with a wounded soul and many voids, God used Ryan to heal me in certain areas of my life and fill some of those empty voids. I am grateful for the encouragement and authentic love Ryan gives me because it brings the motivation I need to keep pursuing and accomplishing my goals in Christ. I consider myself blessed to have a life partner and soul mate who has drawn me closer to Christ. I thank God every day for Ryan; he is truly my best friend.

I am blessed to have three beautiful children who God has used to shape my life and help me discover who I am in Him, even more. Darrin, Ryan, and Rudii have brought forth much purpose in my life. There were times on my journey that I didn't feel worthy, and God used them as my personal confirmation to let me know that I am worthy, and I have value. There is nothing like a mother's love. I am grateful that God chose me to mother, nurture, provide, serve, and love my children. One of the greatest feelings I've encountered and live for is the reciprocated love back from each one of them with a kiss, hug, smile, and sometimes just bright eyes staring at me, connecting with my heart, soul, and spirit. God has truly used my children to awaken the dead areas of my life and heal my wounded soul. My children were God's amazing saving grace to me; they changed the direction of my life and gave me a reason to live. Darrin, Ryan, and Rudii inspire me to keep growing in Christ. I am forever grateful that God trusted me with three beautiful gifts and every day I tell the Lord, "Thank you."

I am very grateful for my grandfather Walter and my dad, Derrick. Both of these men played major roles in my life. They mean the world to me because they stepped up in my life when everyone else stepped out. I am grateful for their love and commitment to see me through life as a troubled teen. Knowing that they have always wanted the best for me truly encouraged me to keep moving forth in life. They have always been there for me, especially during the times I needed them the most. Growing up with the struggle of being neglected, rejected, and abandoned was very heartbreaking. And to feel the acceptance from them was surely a sign from God that He will always have the right people in my path for a purpose. Whenever I needed a shoulder to cry on, a place to vent, or whatever it may be, all I had to do was call. I am grateful for their unconditional love.

To my brothers, Juan and Ricky, I am grateful for the bond we share. I am grateful that when no one understood me, both of you did. You two truly are a sister's love. Our bond has kept me strong on many days when I felt like giving up on life. We share some of the same hurt and pain, but we also share some of the most profound memories that have kept our bond tight and filled with love. I am blessed to have you two as my brothers because I truly know that you both are your sister's keeper, and that is why I love you both. I am blessed to have you both in my life. You two have played a major role in my Spiritual Awakening Journey. Our childhood memories will forever be in my heart. I found so much of my purpose in the bond that we share. I am blessed to be your sister.

To Van, Jeremy, Auntie Barbara, Lil Van, Dewanna, Cheneish, Michael, and Marcus. I want you all to know Grandma, Sylvia, Uncle Van, Dominique, and Brandon would be so proud of the bond that we still share as a family. I am grateful for the bond that has brought much joy and happiness in my life. Each one of you plays a significant role in my journey to becoming whole. I bless God for the unity we have through the foundation that was laid for us as little kids by our grandmother. Those family gatherings were the moments that changed my life. The many Thanksgivings and Christmases we shared as a family were healing to my damaged soul. I am blessed to have my family. Each of you has a special place in my heart.

A special thank you to my Pastor, Perron Daily, my 1st Lady, Prophetess Brandy Daily, and my Green Pasture Church family for supporting the call on my life. I am truly honored to have such dynamic leaders who wholeheartedly lead by example of holiness and righteousness. I am grateful for Pastor and First Lady Daily; they are excellent leaders that God has used to activate and cultivate the call on my life. I am thankful to God for leading my family and me to their ministry because it has truly blessed and reshaped the structure of our lives. God used my leaders to help me give birth to my purpose and to confirm the call as an Evangelist on my life. This book was birthed out of their ministry, and I still remember when my Pastor gave me the prophetic word that I would be an author. The words that were spoken by God through my Pastor are now being manifested. I thank God daily for my leaders and my church home. My family and I are so blessed to be a part of such an amazing, loving, supportive, and life-changing ministry founded on God's Holy Word.

A special thank you to every lady that is a part of The Prayer Summit Ministry. God birthed this ministry through me in 2018, while under the leadership of Pastor and First Lady Daily. God gave me the assignment as midwife and prayer coach to pray with other women and teach them how to pray effectively, along with helping each one of them give birth to their purpose. God has sent me some amazing women who are excited to build a prayer life and get to know God for themselves. I am thankful to God first and foremost for entrusting me with an assignment such as this and also thankful to each lady for trusting the God in me. Their prayers, love, encouragement, commitment, and support have helped me develop who I am in Christ.

Last but not least, to Mother Carter, who God has sent in my life to enrich my spirit man even more. I am forever grateful and endowed by her unconditional love. I am thankful for the Spiritual Mother God has sent me, which has helped filled the many voids of a mother, both naturally and spiritually. I thank God for the Woman of God that she is, the example she sets for me, and for accepting me as her own. She has truly brought forth much joy and assurance from God that I am worthy, I am valuable, I am loved, and I am understood. I am grateful to have an ear that will listen and a heart that will love with no judgment. I consider myself blessed to have her in my life.

May God continue to bless all of these outstanding people that He has used to be a part of my Spiritual Awakening Journey.

Keisha D Haynes

Introduction

A Spiritual Awakening is a collection of prophetic poetry, written in hope to awaken your spirit man with a newfound awareness of your spiritual reality. Spiritual awakenings don't just occur one time. You should always be discovering something new about yourself. Therefore, the newfound awareness or discoveries produce a continued cycle of spiritual awakenings. This continued process produces a zeal, passion, and desire from within to pursue life in its fullness so that your purpose will manifest and you'll become enlightened and transformed into becoming a new and better you in Christ. In order for you to know what God has purposed for you to do in life, understand your purpose, gain the necessary knowledge and revelation to pursue your purpose, and be excited about it you must undergo the continued process of being spiritually awakened.

First and foremost, you must have the knowledge of what it means to be spiritual. Spirituality is simply the connection and revelation gained through the relationship with Jesus Christ. God is a spirit and in order for you to know God, you have to connect with him with a spiritual mind. Each piece that is written is inspired by the different stages of my life that I went through in order for my spirit man to become awakened.

It is necessary that you live a transparent life. You have to constantly examine yourself so that you can accept your truth in order to gain the knowledge needed to transform. I had to go through a series of transparency, which forced me to accept my truth. One thing for sure is if you cannot accept your truth, then you will not be able to accept who you are in God or your purpose. Often times, we tend to run from our truth and cover it up because it can be very painful, hurtful, and even shameful. My relationship with Christ has taught me that the very thing that I was ashamed of is the thing God wanted to use for His Glory. Accepting the hard-core truth of your reality is the first step to your freedom.

As you read this book, it is my heart's desire that you will undergo the experience of being completely broken. After you accept your truth, you have to allow God to break you in order to make you whole. This breaking is not for the natural man, but the spirit man. While your spirit man is constantly becoming spiritually awakened, you have to continue to allow God to spiritually break you from carnality. Carnality opposes spirituality and causes the spirit man to become resistant to spiritual things. If you want to become spiritually enlightened, you have to allow God to feed your spirit with His Holy Spirit. And in order for that to happen, you have to allow God to break you. This breaking produces a hunger and thirst for God and His righteousness like never before. This phase tends to be the most painful because it forces you to let go of everything that is keeping you in bondage. During this breaking, you learn how to forgive others who betray, hurt, reject, and misuse you. You have to learn to love them despite their wrongdoings simply because Jesus loves you despite yours. As humans, it is far too easy to hold onto grudges. We feel as though we have reason to hold onto unforgiveness because of unfair treatment. Not so! That is not true. When we are in bondage, we can't see things the way Christ sees it, because our spirit man is not awakened. In fact, if or when we don't allow God to break us from that way of thinking, we become consumed by sorrow, doubt, insecurities, bitterness, and even hate, which in turn robs us from the joy of life's purpose. Allowing God to break you is necessary so that His light can shine within you. God's light awakens what is on the inside of you and provokes it to come alive.

The light that awakens the spiritual things inside of you that was once lying dormant brings forth a supernatural healing that will only manifest through the outpouring of God's Holy Spirit. To become spiritually awakened is the art of being healed. Once you accept your truth through transparency and allow God to separate you from yourself, to become completely whole in Him. You can then experience healing in your mind, body, and soul that will invoke your spirit man to rise. Often times, people live life spiritually dead because of the pain and agony from the issues of life have numbed them, so they have no desire to live out their purpose. God wants you to pursue your purpose healed and whole. During this healing process, you learn how to love again and how to love others just the way Christ loves you. Healing starts in the soul realm, transfers to the natural, and then entreats the spirit man to come alive, opening your eyes to see things the way Christ does. At this point in your life, you may not know or understand why you are stuck, numb, desensitized, or downtrodden. Perhaps it's because you need supernatural healing through the connection with God. All it takes is just one touch, one encounter with God that will change your life in the most drastic way and bring forth supernatural healing that will spark the passion and drive on the inside of you, awakening your spirit man.

When you are properly healed, you can be restored with an excitement to live out your ultimate purpose in life. This book offers freedom, healing, and deliverance. You do not deserve to live as a captive, in bondage, or stagnated.

Your purpose is not void and your living shall not be in vain. That is why Jesus Christ, our Lord and Savior died, offering us the fulfillment of a whole life.

A spiritual awakening searches the heart of man and provokes healing at its core, bringing forth peace through the Holy Spirit's anointing. There is chaos, confusion, and a lack of love all around you in this world. Isaiah 26:3 tells us that, "Thou wilt keep him in perfect peace, whose mind is stayed on thee: because he trusteth in thee." In other words, as long as you keep your mind on Jesus, He will give you perfect peace - the peace that passes all understanding (Philippians 4:7). In order to know God, you have to learn Him and learn of His ways. In order to learn of His ways, you have to seek Him through prayer and reading His Holy Word. Most importantly, you have to hear him, which requires you to have a life full of peace that can only be found in Him. God is calling you to a life of peace, offering you a sound mind despite the noise that surrounds you.

The poetic writings in this book will bring forth an anointing of peace over your life and the joy that only the Lord can give you. Amongst the pages of this book, you will discover the joy and love that lies within you. Remember, Jesus Christ is Love. John 15:13 says, "Greater love hath no man than this, that a man lay down his life for his friends." Jesus gave you and I the best example of love, dying for us and for those that don't even accept him. In essence, as believers, we are to mimic that same love Jesus has for us to others. God left us with the commandment to love our neighbors as we love ourselves (Mark 12:31). The foundation of joy is love and both are necessary for your spiritual growth to spiritually prosper in life.

I pray that this book heals your soul and enriches your spirit man to come alive so you can flourish in your God-given purpose. May God bless you on your journey to become spiritually awakened. I leave you with my favorite scripture, "You shall love the Lord your God with all your heart and with all your soul and with all your mind" (Matthew 22:37). Allow God's Holy Spirit to dwell within you so you can come alive and live.

inhale

exhale

Born into Brokenness

So, I was the little girl taken from her mom at the tender age of three

because my teenage parents had addictions

that would not allow them to care for me.

My mom was addicted to crack cocaine pretty much all of my life.

My dad suffered from alcoholism, moved out of state, and stayed out of sight.

So, I was a little girl who was raised by her grandparents

who filtered as much love

in me as they could.

But because of mental abuse and neglection,

I suffered from feelings of being unwanted, unloved, and rejection.

As I got older, I realized the effects,

I was the little girl robbed from my identity.

Therefore, I made choices that affected me physically.

Sex before marriage, abortions, STD's, fighting, stealing, and running away.

What more was there to say?

I was searching for something that was never planted in me -

my identity.

The results: at the age of 19, I had a baby. Then at 21, I had another.

Unmarried, two different baby daddies and me not knowing how to be a mother.

Broken. Broken. Broken. A complete mess.

All because I was born into brokenness.

Therefore, I became addicted to everything that was not good for me.

All because I was robbed of my identity.

Clubs, weed, drug dealers, and material things led me astray.

But God and His loved shone on me one day.

He told me, "Just because you were broken at birth,

that doesn't determine your worth."

For you created my inmost being; you knit me together in my mother's womb.
I praise you because I am fearfully and wonderfully made; your works are wonderful,
I know that full well. My frame was not hidden from you when I was made in the
secret place, when I was woven together in the depths of the earth. Your eyes saw my
unformed body; all the days ordained for me were written in your book before one of
them came to be.
Psalm 139:13-16

My Thoughts

"Born into Brokenness" was inspired by transparency as to how and why my life was fashioned in such a way that didn't bring glory to God, yet He still showed me great favor, mercy and produced wholeness in and through me. I had to dig deep to discover how to accept my value and worth given to me by God after all the unhealthy choices I'd made. Through this writing, God revealed to me that the choices I made in life weren't my fault; those choices were the result of being born into a broken environment and being birthed by broken people. Damaged vessels produce damaged vessels and, in my case, my belated mother, Sylvia M. Johnson, and my father, Edward A. Young, were both damaged when I was conceived. Therefore, when I was born, I was damaged. This meant I matured with a damaged state of mind that affected the choices I made. Being a victim of brokenness caused me to make broken decisions. God showed me that just because I was born broken, I didn't have to stay that way. Coming into the knowledge of Christ was the foundation of understanding my true worth.

Your Thoughts

Evaluate your life, including the broken areas that may have caused you to make decisions for which you are not so proud. And know that you are not defined by those decisions. In order for you to become totally free and whole, it is important for you to understand those decisions were the results of brokenness. You made broken choices because imperfection is what lies deep within you and, like me, you didn't ask for it; you were born into it.

Now that you understand that, please take this time to forgive yourself. No longer will you keep blaming yourself for things you had no control over. Allow your brokenness to become the driving force of you are now becoming.

Spoken Word from God to Inspire Your Soul

Journal Prompt

Use the next few pages to journal your thoughts on the following:

What is broken in your life?

Are you living a life of brokenness?

Do you blame yourself? If so, why?

What can you do to go from a life of brokenness to a life of wholeness?

Spoken Word from God to Inspire Your Soul

Sold Out to Christ

Jesus died so that I could have life.

Therefore, I'm all sold out to Christ.

In my darkest days and during the midnight hour,

when I'm weak and weary, He is my strong tower.

The love He has for me is like no other.

It filled all my voids when I was lost and in search of my mother!

Walking this walk! The righteous walk! The holy walk!

I've had to sacrifice.

And it was all worth it, 'cause I'm all sold out to Christ!

I will not turn back to the life of my past.

My mind is made up and I'm free at last!

Free from all the bondage, hurt, pain, rejection, and being misunderstood.

No longer will I allow the enemy to keep robbing me from my livelihood!

'Cause I found Christ! And when I found Christ, I found me.

Free indeed. Indeed, I'm free!

I'm thankful for Jesus Christ, the Son of our living God!

'Cause with them both I beat the odds!

The alpha and omega!

My beginning and my end.

My mind regulator.

My way maker.

My love when I'm hurt.

My joy when I'm in pain.

My peace-of-mind when I thought I was going insane.

I'm telling y'all, I'm all sold out!

See, what I found out is that all my pain was purposed.

Through Christ, all my hurt was healed.

Jesus Christ created in me a new reveal.

Flawed, fearfully and wonderfully made, and perfect in God's eyesight.

That's why I'm all sold out to Christ!

He sees me just as I am, repaired everything broken, healed my soul,

completed me and made me whole.

Loved me in spite of and gave me a sense of worth.

'Cause I was purposed from birth!

I'm God's girl, daughter of the King.

Jesus Christ, you reign! You reign!

And because of who He is, and the blood Jesus sacrificed,

I'm telling y'all I'm totally sold out to Christ.

Jesus answered, "The first and most important one is: 'HEAR, O ISRAEL, THE LORD OUR GOD IS ONE LORD; AND YOU SHALL LOVE THE LORD YOUR GOD WITH ALL YOUR HEART, AND WITH ALL YOUR SOUL(life), AND WITH ALL YOUR MIND (thought, understanding), ANDWITH ALL YOUR STRENGTH.'
Mark 12: 29-130 (AMP)

Spoken Word from God to Inspire Your Soul

My Thoughts

"Sold Out to Christ" is inspired by the authentic, pure love I have for the one living God and Jesus Christ. When I came into the knowledge of Christ and truly understood who I am in God, I couldn't help but fall in love with Him, simply because He first loved me without reason. To understand that God (my Father) sent His only son to die for me so I could have life in an abundance was mind-blowing and the confirmation I needed to know how important and special I was in the eyesight of God. I learned that although life has its ups and downs, and in some cases, more downs than ups, accepting Jesus Christ as my savior positioned me to be a victor, which meant I would never be defeated. Being sold out to Christ is about giving up everything to live a life that pleases the Lord simply because I owe it to Him in exchange for the sacrifices He made for me. I've found the benefits far greater than I ever could have imagined.

Your Thoughts

Are you holding onto hurt, pain, or resentment? Is it robbing you of your joy and peace? My question to you would be: Why? When you have a Father who sent His only begotten Son as a sacrifice for your hurt and pain. We are not promised a painless life, but with God, we are promised a comforter, and that comforter is Jesus Christ. You have to accept him to fully understand and receive the love, restoration, and healing that is promised to you by God. I want to encourage you today to let go of anything and everything that has you bound and give it to the Lord Jesus Christ, becoming totally sold out to Him, giving him all your being. I promise you will experience a greater level of joy, peace, and love. His love is, indeed, matchless.

Spoken Word from God to Inspire Your Soul

Journal Prompt

Use the next few pages to journal your thoughts on the following:

Are you totally sold out to Christ? If not, what's stopping you?

Think of some things you can do and give to become completely sold out.

God Is Trying to Tell You Something

So, you're tired and your back is up against the wall.

Head hung low, weak, drained in spirit and praying that you don't fall.

You've fallen by the wayside, low in the valley, in the desert,

in the deepest ditch!

Begging and pleading with God to get you out of this glitch.

The glitch that has your life in bondage, stagnated, Satan's biggest heist.

You've forgotten that Jesus Christ has already paid the price!

The price for you and me to live free.

The price so we can see who we were created to be!

God is trying to tell you something!

He wants to wipe away all the guilt and shame.

God is trying to tell you something!

Don't listen to all those voices of loved ones telling you,

"You ain't gon' be nothing!"

Listen.

God is trying to tell you something!

He wants more of you.

He wants you to love on Him.

He wants to build you up.

He wants you free in Him.

He wants to elevate your faith.

He wants to open doors man CAN NOT close,

simply because He's the only one who knows.

He knows what it takes to deliver you from evil and set your soul free.

God knows what it takes for you to live happily!

God is trying to tell you something!

Build yourself a prayer life!

Worship Him even the more, 'cause you're the one that He adores.

God is trying to tell you something!

Open your eyes. Focus on the prize.

So that you can realize

that God is trying to tell you something!

Spoken Word from God to Inspire Your Soul

You're a winner in Him.

No longer do you have to live defeated.

Run your race! Don't give up!

Hold on! Don't give in! You're destined to win!

So, listen, God is trying to tell you something!

It's your time! He needs you to rise!

He's waiting to dry up your tears and heal you from those silent cries!

Open your heart. Let Him live in.

Give Him your mind, body, soul – your whole being.

God is trying to tell you something!

Release all that has you consumed. Let go! Live free!

Walk in total obedience and allow God to lead!

He will not lead you astray for His way is the only way!

Repent and be delivered today! That's what God has to say!

So, if the Son makes you free, then you are unquestionably free.

John 8:36

Spoken Word from God to Inspire Your Soul

perfectly imperfect

pg. 46

My Thoughts

"God Is Trying to Tell You Something" is inspired by the intimate relationship I have with God. A relationship built on listening and hearing him to gain self-clarity. I knew that if anyone could lead me out of bondage, it would be the Lord. I could only follow by listening and not solely on passive listening but active listening as well, which means that I learned to listen to receive, with the intent to do what the Lord commands. In order to live free and secure my salvation, I learned to listen. Often times, I went to God and always had something to tell Him, but I never took the time to rest in his presence and hear His responses. The Bible declares in Proverbs 4:7, "that in all my getting to be sure to get an understanding." This scripture gave me the revelation that there was no way I could gain understanding without an ear to hear. "God Is Trying to Tell you Something" is so profound because it speaks to the relationship that I had to develop with Jesus Christ, my Lord and Savior. The intimacy was so imperative because it developed my faith even more and helped me totally trust God and allow Him to be the navigation of my life. Listening is the foundation of flourishing.

Your Thoughts

Think about how many times you only talked to God when you needed Him to get you out of a situation; you needed a bill paid, or you needed healing. You began to cry out and because He's God, He shows up every time with great favor and mercy. Just thinking He will fix every situation doesn't mean you should try to use Him when you want to. Why? Just think about it. If it were you, would you want someone to call you only when they needed you? I'm pretty sure your answer is no. Although God specializes in being sovereign over your life, that doesn't mean you don't need to take the necessary time to rest in His presence and open your spiritual ears to hear the things He has to say. Truth be told, some of the ditches you found yourself so deep in could have been avoided if you took the time to hear God's voice. I've learned that God allows us to fall in ditches so we can understand the imperativeness of a relationship with Him. It is necessary and essential because we can only survive with God. You can only walk in prosperity with God and you can only be totally healed, delivered, and set free with God. Notice I said "with" God, so it's time to stop talking "to" God and start having a conversation with Him. Remember, communicating is the act of talking with and listening.

Journal Prompt

Use the next few pages to journal your thoughts on the following:

Are you conversing with God or to God?

What is God trying to tell you?

Can you hear what He is saying clearly in regard to shaping and forming your life?

Is He telling you to let some things go, so that you can draw closer to him?

Search your heart and soul and allow that small still voice to speak to you?

Restoration

Peace in your mind to think.

Calmness in your spirit to be relieved.

Healing in your body to be made whole.

Strength to rejuvenate your soul.

Recondition your energy.

Visions and dreams then become a reality –

God-given that is!

Serenity to rest,

so you can give God your very best!

Ask Him to cleanse the unclean.

Purify your heart.

Build up what's been torn down.

After all, you deserve a crown.

It's restoration time.

Silence.

Joy flowing like living waters.

Light in the dark.

Healing for your hurt.

A quench for your thirst.

Flames of fire.

Explosions bursting within.

No longer do you have to live in sin,

because restoration begins.

After the shaping and molding there is a process.

Be still and know that He is God, so you can pass the test!

Allow Him to restore you.

Intimacy is what He needs.

Planting the fruit of the spirit in you, those powerful seeds.

Adopt the mindset of Christ,

because it is Him who will change your life.

A servant is who you are.

Pleasing God is what you do.

Righteousness is what you stand for.

Holiness becomes a lifestyle,

because you're God's child.

Restoration. Restoration. Restoration.

Worry, no more.

Because...

God makes all things new.

He restores,

gives sight to the blind,

hearing to the deaf,

life, security, and hope to the broken.

His grace and mercy are sufficient enough.

Indeed, you can count on Him when the going gets tough.

Our God is all-powerful,

all-knowing and seeing,

because He loves you.

He is restoring your spirit and innermost being.

So, get happy.

God has made His way,

to come see about you and me on this day.

And I heard a great voice out of heaven saying, Behold, the tabernacle of God is with men, and he will dwell with them, and they shall be his people, and God himself shall be with them, and be their God.

And God shall wipe away all tears from their eyes; and there shall be no more death, neither sorrow, nor crying, neither shall there be any more pain: for the former things are passed away.

And he that sat upon the throne said, Behold, I make all things new. And he said unto me, write: for these words are true and faithful.
Revelation 21:3-5

My Thoughts

Restoration is the process of being restored. According to the Miriam Dictionary, "restored" means "to bring back to or put back into a former or original state." The synonyms are **RENEW, RESTORE, REFRESH, RENOVATE** and **REJUVENATE**. This process was necessary in order for me to be used by God for the purpose in which I was created. Restoration was the start of my healing process (healing was critical and essential for my mind, body, spirit, and soul). I had to wholeheartedly allow restoration to take place in my life so I could be fully healed from the many things that left me broken, sad, confused, misused, and hurt, with the ending result of feeling hopeless and doubting Gods power. Not only was I hopeless, but I also felt lifeless and unworthy of my purpose and calling. I accepted things that I shouldn't have accepted. I started blaming myself for traumatizing things instead of seeing things from God's perspective. My acceptance of the false reality kept me in bondage and holding onto all the things that were meant to break me. Things that were sent to weaken my faith and doubt God. I had unconsciously put a wedge between my relationship with Abba, my Father. Not knowing that the more I held on to the hurt and pain, the more I lived in pity and the more I separated myself from God.

I didn't realize the state I was in until I decided to allow God to work on me and transform my life. I knew that through it all, God was trying to tell me something. So, I began to read my Bible more, read more Christian books, and listen to sermons. I knew it had to be a better way to live my life than the defeated way I was currently living. One day, I remember laying on my late grandmother's couch watching the Christian channel with tears rolling down my eyes because my grandmother had just died. I was still in search of my identity, dealing with relationship problems, and verbal and mental abuse. I felt rejected my entire life by both parents. I had so much hurt and pain that lay within. I couldn't understand how I could move forward in a life of prosperity and happiness centered around Christ. At that very moment, while crying and listening to the word of God coming across the TV screen, I heard God say to me, "I'm restoring you." He told me to release everything that was hurting me and trust Him with it all. As I began to, I felt healing take place. I started to see things differently and began smiling. I chose to embrace the obstacles that were meant to deter me from my purpose. God told me that those obstacles were meant to show me who He was in my life even more. He cleansed my spirit so that He could shine from within me. He rebuilt me so that I could weather the storms that were necessary to make me everything that God made me to be. During the weathering, He showed me that newness lies ahead. If I endured the trials and held onto His unchanging hand, all would be well. It wasn't until God fully restored me that I was able to truly see life from a different perspective. After being broken, I had to be restored so that I could be made whole.

Your Thoughts

Think about the things that have left you feeling paralyzed, hopeless, and lifeless. Think about the things that you have buried deep down inside - things that have robbed you from the joys of life. Allow God to bring to your remembrance the day you lost your passion, your smile, your zeal, and your excitement to live life on its best terms. Now is the time for you to revisit those things that have stolen your joy and happiness. Revisiting allows God to fully heal and restore (renew, rejuvenate, and refresh) you internally and externally. Let me remind you, God knows all and sees all, so everything that has taken place in your life that has numbed you to the point that you feel unworthy. He knows about it. It's only when you open up to Him that He can breathe on those numb areas and bring them back to life. There is no situation or circumstance too big for God to repair, restore, and rebuild. Don't be afraid to open up and embrace the newness. Allow God to restore you from the inside out because you have a purpose in this life. Don't allow those circumstances or situations to stop you from living your best life in God because you deserve it - simply because God saw you as being worthy. You have to see yourself in the same manner in which God sees you.

Spoken Word from God to Inspire Your Soul

grace

Spoken Word from God to Inspire Your Soul

Journal Prompt

Use the next few pages to journal your thoughts on the following:

From what do you need to be healed?

Will you allow God to restore you?

Do you wholeheartedly trust that God can restore you and replenish your life?

Do you believe that He makes all things new?

Take a deep breath and be in silence for a moment and allow Him to recondition your mind and embrace the process of being restored. Your perspective of life will then change forever. It's time to smile again.

Purification

No more of me, all of you, God!

Reality is what I need; I'm tired of living a facade!

My life is up and down, in and out.

Seems as though I'm always in doubt.

This state of mind I'm in,

I can't seem to win.

Lord, I need you to wash me, cleanse me and purge me.

Let purification kill my flesh

so that I can die to self.

Strip everything from me until there's nothing left

but a will to serve you, a heart to love you, and a mind to worship you!

There's a yes in my soul,

Lord, I want to be made whole!

I'm tired of covering up and pretending that all is well,

living a life full of sin, that's leading me straight to hell!

Lord, I need you to rescue me, arrest my mind, and transform my thinking!

Pick me up Lord, 'cause it feels like I'm sinking.

Purification it is.

Sanctify me Lord, so that you can justify me,

because my life is not my own.

For it is you who sits on the throne.

I surrender my all; then I can stand tall.

Anoint me. Appoint me. Use me for your glory.

Because it is you Lord, who is the author of my story.

Assurance in you and salvation is what I need.

I give myself away, so that you can lead.

Lord I will follow you wherever you tell me to go,

because it is you who knows what my future holds.

The purging, washing, and cleansing is a part of the process.

Although I may not understand,

my hope is in you God, not man.

Purification it is,

There's a price we must all pay.

We must not question You Lord, just follow you all the way.

Thank You, God, is all I have to say.

And no matter how I feel,

I will trust you Lord, because I know you are real.

Pleasing you is all that I desire.

Purify me Lord, so that I can go higher.

THE HIGHER I GO IN YOU, THE LESS OF ME!

PURIFY ME LORD SO THAT I CAN TOTALLY BE FREE!

What does a believer have in common with an unbeliever? What agreement is there between the temple of God and idols? For we are the temple of the living God; just as God said: "I WILL DWELL AMONG THEM AND WALK AMONG THEM; AND I WILL BE THEIR GOD, AND THEY SHALL BE MY PEOPLE. "SO COME OUT FROM AMONG UNBELIEVERS AND BE SEPARATE," says the Lord," AND DO NOT TOUCH WHAT IS UNCLEAN; And I will graciously receive you and welcome you [with favor], And I will be a Father to you, And you will be My sons and daughters," Says the Lord Almighty.

Therefore, since we have these [great and wonderful] promises, beloved, let us cleanse ourselves from everything that contaminates body and spirit, completing holiness [living a consecrated life—
a life set apart for God's purpose] in the fear of God.
2 Corinthian 6:16-18, 7:1

Spoken Word from God to Inspire Your Soul

God has A plan

My Thoughts

"Purification" is inspired by my willingness to live a life pleasing to the Lord. After God restored me, there were a lot of things I had to let go of in order to grow in God and walk in my purpose. I had to let go of everything that had a stronghold over me or had me captive and in bondage. God had to cleanse things that were not pleasing to him. I call the purification process, the removal of all contaminants. God stripped me from everything that was no good for me: clubbing, smoking marijuana, drinking, lying, stealing, sexual relations before marriage, bad attitudes, wrong perceptions, wrong motives, and a negative mindset. If I wanted to get closer to God, I had to be purged and purified. Every last one of those things kept me far away from His presence. In order for the Lord to dwell in me and work through me, it was imperative that I allowed God to purify me for His glory. This included separating me from friends that He knew didn't meant me well, the ones He knew that would betray me. In essence, it all worked out for my good. The purification process doesn't feel good because it's done through an act of obedience. Not my will, but God's. I knew that in order to get all God had for me, I had to let go of all the hindering and truly allow him to saturate me with His spirit. The purging was very uncomfortable, but it was necessary. Somethings hurt more than others to let go, but it was necessary to discover that the purification process was the foundation of God's Glory shining through my life. God's light couldn't shine through a dirty vessel.

Your Thoughts

Please understand that God isn't forceful and He will not force purification on you. This process is done through your obedience, simply because you trust Him. Remember, He knows what is best for you. After all, He is the creator of your life and if you want to live it pleasing the Lord, this process is necessary. Holding onto the ungodly things stops you from being one with God. Please understand that the light within you remains dim until you remove all the contaminants. There is no better feeling than being in tune with God. Without being purified, it is impossible.

Journal Prompt

Use the next few pages to journal your thoughts on the following:

What are the things that are hindering your relationship with your father?

Identify the things that you know are affecting your spiritual growth. Ask yourself the question, is it really worth it?

Are you willing to go through the painful process of being purified so you can be in right standing with the Lord? Are you okay with being stuck?

Faith Your Miracle

I heard a loud voice that came from above saying,

"Be still and know that I am God. Your battle has already been won!

So, hold on and never give in.

While you're walking with me, the enemy shall never win!

I know it seems as though I'm nowhere to be found;

trust me sons and daughters; I will never let you down.

Every word I speak is truth.

What I say gives you life.

You can't throw in the towel; you must continue to fight!

Fight with your faith.

Believe what seems unbelievable.

Allow patience to have its perfect works and watch me move the unmovable.

Faith your miracle is what I said!

Worry about nothing,

because it is I who gives you your daily bread!

No more suffering and no more sorrow;

take no thought about the cares of tomorrow.

Don't get tired now; you've come too far to leave.

No matter how it looks, just believe! Believe! Believe!

Faith your miracle.

Stand on my Word, submit to my Will and follow my Way,

because Jesus Christ rose and He has already paid.

Paid for it all. Paid for the sins.

No condemnation, therefore, destiny wins.

He was bound and chained, but yet set you free,

so humble yourself and live graciously.

I am the burden Barrier,

the heavy load Carrier,

the mind regulator, peace during the storm.

I mend broken vessels that have been shattered and torn.

I know all. I see all.

It is you I called and with my Spirit, you can stand tall!

The Trinity (Father, Son, and Holy Spirit) is all that you need.

Let go of your past and just follow my lead.

The only way from here is up

and that you must believe.

You got to faith your miracle because you've been redeemed.

Faith your miracle!

And Jesus said unto them, Because of your unbelief: for verily I say unto you, If ye have faith as a grain of mustard seed, ye shall say unto this mountain, Remove hence to yonder place; and it shall remove; and nothing shall be impossible unto you.
Matthew 17:20

My Thoughts

"Faith Your Miracle" is inspired by the level of faith I had to develop on my personal journey of walking with God. I learned that in order to overcome situations that seemed hard to conquer and to see the manifestations of God, I had to trust God wholeheartedly. My faith walk taught me that the power of faith will cause the supernatural to manifest. One of the scriptures I kept near and dear to my heart was Hebrews 11:6, which states, "Without faith, it is impossible to please God." Through that scripture, God gave me a revelation: faith is the active ingredient that will cause God's hand to move in my life. I needed to have full faith in God in order for me to first, be pleasing to Him, and second, to witness His power. I now understand that in life, there will always be tests and trials, but having faith in God is the assurance that all will be well. It is one thing to say you have faith in God, but it is a whole different entity to actually embody the gift of faith and allow it to govern the decisions you make. I have this saying that "faith raised me," because having faith matured me in areas of my life that I would never have grown in if I didn't grab hold to faith and the understanding that there is no problem, circumstance, or situation too big or hard for God to solve. Faith will cause mountains to move. And that is the guaranteed victory promised to me by allowing faith to permeate.

Your Thoughts

I am sure there are areas in your life where you struggle with your faith in God, causing you to hold onto things and situations you need to give up. Once you decide to follow Christ and live for Him, faith is a necessity. Faith is needed for you to grow in God and come to the realization that you cannot do anything without God. If God is your source, then why is it when situations don't work out or you've fallen short, you get upset, worry, and have feelings of unworthiness and being defeated? This is why having faith is essential. Because when things are out of your reach, you can rest in God with the assurance of your faith in Him, knowing that He will sustain and provide. You have to fully understand that faith is a choice you have to consciously make when you allow God to lead. Doing so can be very difficult at times, especially when you are used to having control and working your own problems out. Walking with Christ is a blind walk. 2 Corinthians 5:7 declares that "We walk by faith but not by sight." In other words, even when you don't understand or see how, faith says God has it all worked out. That is why you must choose faith; because it is your faith that will activate God's promises to you. You indeed have to "faith your miracle" because that is the only way it will manifest.

Spoken Word from God to Inspire Your Soul

Set free
Galatians 5:4

pg. 82

Spoken Word from God to Inspire Your Soul

Journal Prompt

Use the next few pages to journal your thoughts on the following:

Do you have faith? How do you know?

How do you respond to the challenges in life?

Can you grow stronger in your faith? How?

Spoken Word from God to Inspire Your Soul

The Sacrificial Life

A sacrificial life is one that is hidden in Christ.

With a lifestyle of worship and a heart full of praise,

fervent prayers and meditation are what gets you through the days.

The days that are filled with brokenness, loneliness, and depression.

The days that are full of heartaches, headaches, and disappointments.

Battling in the mind, the thoughts to overcome the rejection.

It's those prayers, y'all.

Constantly communing with Jesus Christ cause He's your all.

It is Him who encourages you to stand tall.

Reminding you that every obstacle is a lesson.

Therefore, you must never have any regrets and keep pressing,

assured that your life is a complete blessing.

The sacrificial life you live,

your livelihood you give.

Why?

'Cause Jesus Christ is real.

If He can do it for you, you can do it for Him.

Sacrifice. Sacrifice. Sacrifice your life.

Give your all. Do not be afraid to fall.

Sacrificing everything about you because you're called.

So willingly surrender and give him your all,

a sacrificial life you must live, your livelihood you must give.

Determination and dedication to stay in the race,

by constantly staying on your knees and seeking His face.

The turmoil, afflictions, purging, and pain,

sometimes has you feeling like you're going insane.

That is when you know to call His name.

Jesus.

And He answers and says,

"I know it never feels good,

the sacrificial life is one that's often misunderstood.

But be encouraged because it all works together for your good."

The shaking, molding, crushing, and making, is what humbles you, and forms you into who God created you to be.

So therefore, you must live faithfully, carefully giving Him all the glory.

Patiently wait as He orchestrates your story.

He's jealous for you. You have to thirst for Him.

So, the sacrificial life is the life you must choose to live.

"For whoever wants to save their life will lose it,
but whoever loses their life for me will save it."
Luke 9:24

My Thoughts

"The Sacrificial Life" is inspired by the understanding I gained during the season of my life when I had to make constant sacrifices in order to walk one with Christ. I had to change how I lived, how I reacted to certain situations, and, most importantly, my thoughts. I had to sacrifice my human nature for a Godly nature, exchanging my thoughts for God's thoughts, and my will and desires for God's. I realized I was consumed by my human nature to please my flesh, which was in turn, delaying God's plan for my life. Sacrificing was not easy. I had to reprogram myself and constantly die to myself daily, which meant I had to kill my flesh so that I could grow more spiritually. I had to stop arguing with people, even though at times I was right, and instead, take a more peaceful and positive approach to gain a better result. I had to put down bad habits that were leading me astray so that I could be in right standing with God. When I started sacrificing for God, my perspective changed, my attitude changed, my emotions became more controlled, and I developed a more disciplined life. Spiritually, I became more in tune with the voice of God. As I stated earlier in this text, sacrificing isn't easy at all, but with the help of the Holy Spirit, the power of God, a made-up mind to please God, and a heart to serve God, it can be done.

Your Thoughts

Sacrificing is one of the hardest things for humans to do because we become so accustomed and complacent to the ways we live and how we handle situations. When we are conditioned to operate one way, it can be very difficult to recondition ourselves. Therefore, we stay content in the state we're in and end up missing out on our purpose. When it comes to the things of God, change is necessary and in order to change, we have to be willing to make sacrifices. This means we have to give up everything that's valuable to us (materials, views, relationships, food, etc.). Sacrificing is a way of communicating to God, letting him know that nothing is more important than Him, and we are willing to give up any and everything for His sake. After all, our lives are not our own. Our lives belong to God. Therefore, it's imperative to make the necessary sacrifices to ensure Him that we live to please Him. Suffering and sacrificing go hand and hand. One can't be done without the other. So, if you are going to suffer for Christ, you may as well sacrifice for Christ so that God's perfect plan can manifest in your life.

Sacrifice may not feel good to the flesh, but it's definitely necessary for your spirit so you can gain a more intimate relationship with God. Take this time to meditate and evaluate those things you need to release. Listen to that small, still voice and hear what God is asking you to sacrifice for His sake.

Spoken Word from God to Inspire Your Soul

God sees you

Journal Prompt

Use the next few pages to journal your thoughts on the following:

What is it that you feel you need to let go of that is causing you to become complacent?

Do you need to get rid of negative thoughts, stop watching negative TV shows that are clouding your reality about life?

Do you need to end a toxic relationship that is full of negative energy, opposing everything God is saying about your life?

Do you need to sacrifice bad food choices, even though it tastes good because your health is affected (we know that it is God's desire that we prosper with good health)?

What things do you need to release? Why have you held on to them?

Can you hear God speaking to you? What is He saying?

Spoken Word from God to Inspire Your Soul

The Worship Experience

It is your worship that sets the atmosphere.

It is your worship that breaks the curse.

It is your worship that gives you peace.

Your worship causes you to live victoriously.

It is your worship that frees you from bondage;

your worship that gives you the intimacy you need.

'Cause you believe...

when you need a healing... you worship.

When you want joy... you worship.

When you're looking for a miracle... you worship.

Your faith says worship.

Your worship fills you up, draws you closer to dwell in His presence,

opens your heart to love on Him even the more.

The Lord Jesus Christ, 'cause it is Him that you adore...

True worship sets your soul free, opens your eyes to see

that everything He spoke about you, His words you can believe.

Your faith says worship....

For He is the way, the truth, and the life.

Your worship is given as a sacrifice.

Your mind is regulated through worship.

Poverty ends in worship.

Wealth begins in worship.

Oh! It is all about your worship.

Thanking Him for the wonders He has performed,

'cause He carried you through every single storm.

Never did He leave you, nor forsake you.

He picked you up, wiped you off, and paid the cost

so that you can worship.

Obtaining the life of abundance,

obtaining the life of more than enough;

and when times get rough... you worship.

Your worship will change your life.

True encounters with God, the Lord, and Savior Jesus Christ.

Worship Him in spirit and truth, honoring Him with your all.

And loving on Him 'cause He first loved you

Center your lifestyle around worship…

Love Him, adore Him, breathe Him and glean to Him. Make it personal,

strengthen your relationship with Him through your worship.

"But a time is coming and is already here when the true worshipers will worship the Father in spirit [from the heart, the inner self] and in truth; for the Father seeks such people to be His worshipers. God is spirit (the Source of life) and those who worship Him must worship in spirit and truth."
John 4:23-24

Spoken Word from God to Inspire Your Soul

My Thoughts

"The Worship Experience" is inspired by the love and commitment I have for God, my Lord and Savior. The gratitude that I have for Him is displayed through my worship. The thankfulness in my heart for who He is and all that He has done for me, I display it through worship. When I learned the power of worship and how it was a display of my love for the Lord and how it provokes God to move in my life even more, my desire to worship Him increased. I began to worship more freely. When I first began worshipping, I would only worship God for who He is and what He's done for me. Not knowing that worshipping Him for the things I was believing Him to do in my life was imperative for the manifestations of the things I desired. As I matured in my Christian walk, I learned that worshipping Him is an act of my faith and moves the heart of God. Worshipping God by faith changed the way I worshipped. "Faith is the substance of things hoped for, the evidence of things not seen," (Hebrews 11:1). I went from worship to having worship experiences. The craving from the depths of my soul, and the innermost parts of my being, desired to worship God.

Your Thoughts

Worship is your gratitude for the Lord, Jesus Christ, your Savior. It is your shown appreciation to God for simply *being* God. In order to truly worship God, you must first acknowledge that you are nothing without Him. You have to take a look at your life and realize you've only made it this far because of God. When you ponder on the dark places He has brought you out of and the low valleys He has pulled you up from, a desire to give Him thanks should arise from within. The foundation of worship is your appreciation of God's Agape and relentless love because it is matchless and limitless. Know that your worship has to be done through faith. There are things that the Lord desires to manifest to you in your future, but can only be released by faith. There will be times that you do not feel like worshipping. That is why faith is an essential part of your worship experience.

Journal Prompt

Use the next few pages to journal your thoughts on the following:

Now, begin to think about God's goodness and the fact that He has a purpose for you. Yield to the spirit of worship. Allow it to rise from the core of your being. Remember that your love for God and your faith in Him is the driving force of your worship.

Do you know your purpose? What is it and how do you know?

If you aren't certain of your purpose, what are your passions?

Redemption

Simply because I'm covered by His blood and empowered by His love,

I'm set free.

I've been redeemed.

Away from the shackles.

Away from the chains.

They've kept me in bondage, feeling like I was insane -

that pain!

That pain sometimes seemed like it wouldn't go away.

The hurt from it led me astray.

Often, "Jesus" would be the only word I could say!

Strongholds in mind captivating all of my thoughts,

telling me I'll never be free!

Those lies!

Jesus was crucified on Calvary for me; agony it seemed!

He did it simply so that I could be redeemed.

His indescribable and immeasurable love rescued me

from this worldly slavery.

Therefore, I'm no longer guilty -

guilty of the sin, I'm freed from it all.

No reason to feel ashamed, the condemnation is wiped away.

I'm free.

I'm redeemed.

I'm delivered.

I'm loved.

My joy and my peace come from the heavens above.

Everything my God has promised me is mine!

Simply because I believe.

I can and I will obtain it all!

I've been redeemed.

I'm no longer the same now that I realize who's I am and I'm free.

I can now share my story so God will get all the glory.

His light now shines within me, because I live righteously.

Spoken Word from God to Inspire Your Soul

I've been redeemed.

I've been shaken and I have been torn.

Now that I'm free in Christ, I'm reborn.

Time to live out my freedom, because Jesus Christ paved the way.

My old has passed away, for today is a new day

I'm redeemed.

I have total victory.

I'm reborn.

My God sent His only begotten son.

I'm free,

because my Savior, Jesus Christ, loves me.

He has delivered us from the domain of darkness and transferred us to the kingdom of his beloved Son, in whom we have redemption, the forgiveness of sins.

Colossians 1:13-14

My Thoughts

Coming to the knowledge that Jesus redeemed me from the bondage of sin and slavery to this world brought forth unexplainable freedom that rose from within. There have been times in my spiritual walk that I held onto the things of my past and found myself allowing those things to guide my future. The enemy tried his best to control me by using my past experiences as a thief and a liar, telling me that God wouldn't use me because of the wrong decisions I made in life. I had children out of wedlock and the enemy wanted me to believe that I would never get married. Oh, but through the redemption of Jesus Christ, none of those things mattered. My sins were forgiven by God. My slate was wiped clean and God freed me from those reckless thoughts and proved the devil as a liar. Knowing that Jesus sent redemption for me, brought forth a conviction from the heart to want to live for Him. Knowing that I have been forgiven for all the bad and wrong decisions I made, opened my heart to the love of Jesus Christ even the more. I thought if Jesus loved me enough to pay for my sins and I wouldn't be charged for them, then He must truly love me. His redemption truly displayed His unconditionally love for God's people (1 John 3:16). I stopped beating myself up (self-condemnation) when I learned that Jesus Christ paid the ransom for all the wrong I'd ever done. I then started accepting the freedom in forgiveness from God. The redemption of Jesus Christ gave me a reason to live again. "All things work together for the good to those who love God, to them who are called according to His purpose," (Romans 8:28). Jesus' redemption is the foundation of my purpose.

Your Thoughts

Think about the things that are holding you captive. The mistakes you've made and the habits and addictions you can't seem to let go of that are robbing you from your destiny in God. You have to know and believe that there is hope in the redemption of Jesus Christ. You have to understand that His reason for giving His life for yours was so you can be free from bondage. You cannot allow your mistakes, shortcomings, nor your bad decisions dictate your freedom in God. You have to grab hold of your freedom through the forgiveness of God. God loves you, which is why He sent His one and only son to redeem you from the darkness of the world. What am I saying? That there is liberty from whatever has you in bondage, whether it is a toxic relationship, an addiction, bad health, or stinking thinking... there is hope, and that hope is the redemption of Jesus Christ. Often times, the enemy will try to get you thinking that you are in too deep and nothing will ever change but know that Satan is the father of all lies. Nothing is too hard for God or too big for Him to solve. That's why He sent Jesus to solve all the problems He knew you and I would have. I want you to grab hold of your redemption and receive the freedom that provokes you to breakthrough, strongholds and barriers. This freedom will launch you into your purpose. You were bought and paid for by Jesus Christ. You belong to him.

Spoken Word from God to Inspire Your Soul

grateful

pg. 112

Spoken Word from God to Inspire Your Soul

Journal Prompt

Use the next few pages to journal your thoughts on the following:

Make a list of the things that have held you captive. Are they real or imagined?

If they are imagined, let them go and create a new reality.

If they are real, decide how to free yourself from the consequences of your mistakes.

What can you do to live a life from the perspective of freedom?

Created to Birth

My God, you are simply amazing

to choose little 'ole me to give birth to reality.

My God, you are simply amazing;

the way you structured the process.

Months of unrest,

from conception to birth,

enduring pains that were caused by the curse.

Yeah, I know I was created to birth, months and months of sacrifice,

so that I can bring forth life!

What you formed in heaven will manifest through me on earth

because I was created to birth.

Give birth to life. Give birth to visions. Give birth to dreams.

Just as Jesus gave birth to ministry! So, what does that mean?

To some of you, it may seem as though you cannot conceive.

God said, "Continue to trust me. Only if you believe."

Spoken Word from God to Inspire Your Soul

Miscarry.

God said, "Fret not. Continue to tarry."

Birth defects.

God said, "Don't worry. I will give you perfect rest."

Labor pain.

God said, "Keep pushing. Everything around you is about to change!"

You were created to birth.

You were created to produce life.

You were created to bring forth purpose.

Therefore, be encouraged.

Know that the pain is worth it.

Remember, God's plans for your life are perfect!

YOU WERE CREATED TO BIRTH IT!

"I am come that they might have life, and that they might have it more abundantly."
John 10:10

My Thoughts

"Created to Birth" is inspired by the understanding that came after I gained the knowledge of the redemption of Jesus Christ. Knowing that Jesus Christ paid a price so that I could live not only gave me insight into the depth of His love for me but also made me ponder on the "Why?" God revealed to me because I have a purpose. Jeremiah 29:11 declares, "For I know the plans I have for you, declares the Lord plans to prosper you and not to harm you, plans to give you hope and a future." That scripture was my confirmation that the redemption of Jesus Christ is the foundation of my purpose. Jeremiah 29:11 was my reminder that although I was "Born into Brokenness," nothing that took place in my life was intended to harm me. God's plan for my life was to prosper me and give me hope and a good future because I have a purpose. I then began to search for my purpose and came to the realization that God gave me the authority to birth it.

The dreams and visions the Lord gave me were only for me and in order for them to manifest, I had to birth them. So, in other words, I was "Created to Birth." This meant, when God gives me insight on the good future He has for me, I have to grab hold to it by faith (everything that manifests on this earth has to first come through conception [notion, idea, view, image]). I learned that faith was the key that unlocked the potential in me and is the key to unlock the doors of my purpose. Without faith, the vision and dreams (purpose) cannot, and will not, manifest. Hebrew 11:6 declares, "Without faith, it is impossible to believe God." What is faith? Hebrews 11:1 defines it "as the substance of things hoped for, and the evidence of things that are not seen." What things? I learned that those things are my purpose. I had to grab hold to the concept of my purpose from God and bare them with faith, just as I would a baby. Coming into the knowledge that I was created to birth my purpose drove me closer to God.

The relationship between Him and I during this process was essential because baring things that seemed impossible sometimes caused my faith to waiver. During the baring stages (carrying the conception), I learned it was necessary to lean on God to gain the insight I needed to keep carrying. I didn't want to abort my purpose; therefore, seeking God was vital for me. This part of the process is where I gained my strength, endurance, stamina, and comfort to keep believing when I felt like giving up and began to feel the labor pains as I came close to giving birth. After I bared the conception for a time, God told me when it was time to push. This is when He (not I) was ready to manifest my purpose to me even the more. There has been and will be plenty of times that God will take me through the process of giving birth because my purpose isn't just one thing. I was "Created to Birth" the life God planned for me as it relates to my children, marriage, family, business, and ministry.

Your Thoughts

I want you to think about the things God created you to birth. What is your purpose? It has to be something, or else you wouldn't be sitting here reading this book. There are some things that God wants to manifest on this earth through you. Jesus Christ's redemption is your proof that God not only loves you but has also given you a purpose. You are still alive today because there are some things only you can do. Perhaps it's a ministry to help save souls and witness to people about the love of Jesus Christ and sharing your testimony. Or, it may be to help the youth because you have a passion for children. It could be to open a business and give back to the community. Or to raise a happy, loving family. My point is that you have a purpose and you were created to birth it. John 10:10 is your confirmation. That scripture tells you that Jesus Christ came so that you can have life and have it abundantly. In other words, Jesus Christ's purpose was to give you purpose. First, you have to believe it, then seek God for it and be willing to bear it until God is ready for you to manifest it. During the process of discovering your purpose, your relationship with God is necessary, because that is the only way that you can grab hold to the vision. You can only bare it with faith by maintaining a healthy relationship with God. John 10:10 informs you that the enemy's purpose is to kill, steal, and destroy the very thing you are supposed to birth. When you are connected to God, the enemy has no chance. I encourage you today to spend some time with God. Seek Him to understand your purpose. Ask him to show you what it is that you were "Created to Birth."

Spoken Word from God to Inspire Your Soul

pg. 122

Spoken Word from God to Inspire Your Soul

Journal Prompt

Use the next few pages to journal your thoughts on the following:

Your purpose is anything you'd do for free, simply because you love it and you're good at it. Do you know your purpose?

Are you living in your purpose?

Even if your purpose is not how you earn your living, you can still operate in it.

How can you take your purpose to the next level?

Spoken Word from God to Inspire Your Soul

The Transfiguration

Transfigured. Transformed. I've been reborn.

I am now an ambassador of Christ.

I've relinquished the rights to my life.

I am no longer the same.

The glory of God fell upon me one day and everything changed.

I was given a new mind to think and a new way to talk.

God's light showed me a new path to walk.

He distorted my perception of reality

and altered what I can see.

I once was blind, but now I see.

His word is a lamp to my feet, guiding me.

Alone time with God was necessary for me to pursue -

moments that transfigured my inner core and transformed me brand new.

Prayer at the mountaintop,

without ceasing, nonstop!

Fervent, effectual prayers that availed much.

It only takes one touch!

That touch purified my soul,

and made me whole.

God is my master and I am now His sheep.

I've been transfigured into a beautiful masterpiece.

My spirit man has been made alive,

the radiance of God's glory transcended through me and now I'm revived!

No longer is my spirit dull and dim.

Jesus Christ is the light that is bright and shines from within.

I've been purified,

because I am now justified!

What people use to see they don't see any more,

because I have been transfigured. Therefore, I'm transformed.

Therefore, if anyone is in Christ, he is a new creation. The old has passed away; behold, the new has come.
2 Corinthians 5:17

My Thoughts

Transfiguration is a complete change of appearance into a more beautiful or spiritual state. It is a beautiful experience because it confirms that one has allowed God to transform them. After the decision to follow Christ, we must allow God to make us completely new. 2 Corinthians 5:17 says, "Therefore, if anyone is in Christ, he is a new creature; the old things passed away; behold, new things have come." God is constantly making us new through the transfiguration process. Jesus Himself had to undergo this experience (Mark 9:2), to manifest the glory of God on His life. Not only is this experience beneficial for all believers, but it is also beneficial for others to witness the manifestations of God's glory through God's chosen vessel. It helps restore their faith.

I've learned, as a believer, it is very important that I have this experience with God over and over again through prayer, reading His Word, and listening to His quiet, still voice. Transformation is necessary in order to be made in the image of Christ. I had to learn to yield willingly and obediently to the things of God and allow God to transfigure me into the women He called me to be. Not my will, but God's will be done. When I allowed God's will to be done in and through me, that was the start of my transfiguration experience. Just as a caterpillar has to go through the transfiguring stages to become a beautiful butterfly, then so must I. The very beginning of undergoing this process wasn't the easiest because I had to allow God to reshape me. I had to deny myself and de-attach myself from things and people that were no good for my spirit man. I had to destroy my old mindset of fear, anger, doubt, and distrust and allow God to give me a new mind. I found myself praying Psalms 51:10 often. "God create in me a clean heart and renew in me the right spirit." As time went on, yielding to the transfiguration became easier to the point that people witnessed the change that only God could have done. People told me they could see the glory of God shining through me. This was because I allowed God to transfigure me. He changed the way I walked, the way I talked, and how I thought. In essence, He changed my entire personality and appearance, so it produced the radiance of God's glory on my entire life.

Your Thoughts

When it comes to undergoing the transfiguration process, think about the things you are attached to that don't give God the full glory for your life. There are some things that you are holding onto that are dimming your light. God cannot shine through a dark vessel. The only way for you to do away with those wrong thoughts, motives, attitudes, and self-will is to allow God to transfigure you. God has to completely transform you through a lifestyle of prayer, fasting, reading His Word, seeking His face, and listening to Him. God wants to use you as the vessel to display His glory, but it can't be done if you don't undergo the transfiguration process. Matthew 16:24 says, "Jesus said to His disciples, "If any of you wants to be my follower, you must give up your own way, take up your cross, and follow me." In other words, if you are a believer, you must deny yourself in order to be a follower Christ. The more you deny yourself, the more your life represents Christ; therefore, God can shine His glory on you.

Philippians 2:5 tells us, as believers, to have the same mind of Christ. There is no way this can be done without having a transfiguration experience. When this experience takes place in your life, it changes your entire being. Your perception changes, God renews your mind, and He changes your thoughts. He pours out His spirit on you. Therefore, you gain wisdom, knowledge, and understanding of God and His word even more. You find a newfound love for Jesus Christ, your Savior. The transfiguration experience is life-changing, and it is very evident to those that are around you. Your transfiguration experience could be the confirmation to those around you that God is real. When others see everything about you has changed, it encourages them to believe for their change. The beauty of this experience is that it manifests two-fold. First, it has a lasting effect on you. Second, it affects those around you. As I've often said, the change from a caterpillar to a butterfly manifests through the transfiguration experience. I challenge you to take on the same nature as the caterpillar and go through the necessary stages of transformation to produce the glory of God shining in and through you. His radiance is beauty all by itself.

Spoken Word from God to Inspire Your Soul

Journal Prompt

Use the next few pages to journal your thoughts on the following:

Does your life align with Christ's plan now that you've been changed?

How is your life different now that you've been transformed?

What are the good things about being new?

What are some challenging things about transformation?

Spoken Word from God to Inspire Your Soul

Spoken Word from God to Inspire Your Soul

grace

pg. 136

Purpose Driven

God created you for purpose, distinctly and uniquely,

not just to merely survive, but to thrive!

Therefore, be ambitious, determined, with a motivational drive.

From within,

conquer the obstacles of life in order to win.

Let go of all insecurities and live courageously for Jesus Christ.

God created you for a purpose – to live life.

You were built to be brilliant, authentic, and without fear.

Walk in that knowledge – persevere!

Be driven by your purpose,

discover what it is, and live.

Grab hold to your DESTINY by embracing your OPPORTUNITIES.

Unlock your POTENTIAL, relinquish your past.

Accept your FREEDOM and remove the mask.

God created you for a purpose.

Spoken Word from God to Inspire Your Soul

Fearfully and wonderfully, discover the new you.

Underneath your brokenness is someone brand new.

The one that is hidden underneath all the misfortune and rejection.

That's not you - those are false perceptions.

Your failures do not define you and your circumstances do not limit you.

Those barriers you must PUSH through!

God uses those challenges as narratives for your story.

He orchestrates them profoundly for His Glory!

God has a purpose for YOU.

He wants to reveal the unknown. Ignite your fire

with a DESIRE

to Live on purpose and be driven – never to tire.

"For by him all things were created, in heaven and on earth, visible and invisible, whether thrones or dominions or rulers or authorities—all things were created through him and for him."
Colossians 1:16

My Thoughts

The inspiration behind this piece is the drive that came alive within me once I saw the revelation from God as He began to reveal to me pieces of my purpose. Yes! I said "pieces" because I am still discovering that there is more. The manifestations of my purpose came during those moments when I yielded to God and let Him totally transfigure me, through the outpouring of His Holy Spirit. God's spirit ignited a burning fire and desire from within and provoked me to want to love and live for Jesus Christ more. The desire to live for Jesus Christ brought forth a conviction to let go of my will. Through these sacrifices, God manifested my true calling. My purpose was made manifest. I ultimately discovered that my purpose is to live a life of servanthood for the Lord. I understood God needed willing vessels that He can hold accountable and depend on to fulfill His mission on this earth. I said, "yes" to the call of servanthood. That "yes" brought forth so many open doors, unfamiliar doors that led me to my purpose. I embarked on some completely new opportunities that brought forth a great indescribable joy like no other. I found myself very passionate about things I would have never thought that I'd have an interest. Discovering the unknown changed the way I perceived life. It changed the way I lived my life. I went from just living day by day, to living on purpose and being driven by it.

Your Thoughts

Have you discovered your purpose, the uniqueness of your individuality? Discovering your purpose can only be found through a relationship with God. Discovering your purpose is essential because it's the foundation for success. It is the driving force you need to stay motivated to keep moving forward and accomplishing your goals.

Journal Prompt

Use the next few pages to journal your thoughts on the following:

Take a look within. Think about what is holding you back.

What is keeping you stuck and stagnated?

Why are you not moving forward?

Why is your purpose not the driving force navigating you through life?

Spoken Word from God to Inspire Your Soul

Spoken Word from God to Inspire Your Soul

Spoken Word from God to Inspire Your Soul

Spoken Word from God to Inspire Your Soul

The Lord is the strength of my life

Conclusion

God created you for a purpose. Jeremiah 29:11 says, "For I know the plans I have for you, declares the LORD, plans to prosper you and not to harm you, plans to give you hope and a future." Those very words are God's confirmation that you have a purpose. Discovering your purpose will cause you to prosper and give you the hope you need to keep moving forward in life. God created you to make a difference in the lives of His people. God created you to be a change agent. God specially created you to do what nobody else can do. That's why He created you to do it. As you draw closer to Him, you will discover more of who you are in him. During that process, let Him transfigure you. Remember, He is the potter and you are the clay. You have to allow Him to mold you into His purpose. Once that purpose has been made manifest through the outpouring of His Holy Spirit, you become activated, fueled, and charged with a burning desire from within. Experiencing a zeal that will drive you through life and excitement to do what God has called you to do. It is time to awaken the inner you and be completely transformed and renewed. Let your light shine. God is depending on you.

About the Author

Keisha D. Haynes was born and raised in Saint Louis, Missouri by her beloved grandmother who passed in 2009. Insisting that Keisha be led by the Lord, her grandmother had her baptized at the age of 9. Keisha attended Sunday school on a regular basis and was an active member of Greater Bethlehem Baptist Church under the leadership of Dr. Reverend Cleophus Robinson Sr. She served on the usher board, sang in the choir, praised, danced, and opened Sunday School Services. Keisha's grandmother was the greatest inspiration in her relationship with God. Her grandmother inspired her to be a woman of class and showed her the ways of a good wife and the importance of maintaining a home. Most importantly, she learned how important family bonds are.

Keisha is a woman inspired and motivated by God's grace to carry out the purpose upon her life to love all people as Christ loves her. Keisha is very passionate and finds happiness in the fulfillment of life and the world around her. Keisha wears many hats, but the most important is seen through the time she spends communing in God's presence and spending time with her devoted husband, Walter Haynes, and their three beautiful children, Darrin (17), Ryan (14), and Rudii (5). She is faithful, loving, hardworking, and highly motivated about her walk with God.

At the age of 15, Keisha discovered a talent for braiding hair by practicing on family and friends. This catapulted Keisha into a career in the cosmetology industry where she is known for her drive, passion, and creativity. After graduating from McCluer Senior High School in 2001, Keisha enrolled in Elaine

Stevens Cosmetology College. She graduated with her CA in Cosmetology and Manicuring, thereby beginning her career in the Cosmetology industry. She has not taken for granted the favor God has given that sustains her career as a stylist by allowing her to enter hair shows and opening and operating a hair salon in 2010 called "Beauty 4 Ashes" as Master Stylist. She has spent countless hours managing, mentoring, and training upcoming professionals. Keisha is an overcomer, achieving some of life's hardest goals while surviving many hurtful tragedies. Through it all, she continues to strive for the best and stay humble, steadfast, and grateful while continuing to eagerly give God the glory.

Another of Keisha's accolades includes receiving her AAS Degree in Human Services in 2010 at Florissant Valley Community College. She studied humanitarianism while attending various leadership training seminars and interning as a mentor and tutor to many students. In 2013, Keisha obtained her BAS from Fontbonne University of St. Louis, Mo. With the motivation of her devoted husband, Ryan, they made the conscious decision to pursue fashion merchandising and launched their "Fearless Styling Studio" in 2014. Having zeal while learning throughout this time, she realized God was showing her who she was. Being passionate about prayer, Keisha began her prayer ministry group in 2018, originally called "The Sisterhood," and being led by God; she recently changed the name to "The Prayer Summit." In 2018, Keisha and Ryan saw there was a need for children to be nurtured and educated into who God created them to be and opened "Purpose Driven Homeschool Academy."

On December 31, 2019, Keisha entered the new year officially ordained as Evangelist Keisha Haynes. This was a very humbling experience, allowing Keisha a true divine revelation as to why her life was orchestrated in such a manner. She began to understand even more that the call on her life was greater than she could ever imagine. Her mission is to travel the world, preaching the Gospel in hopes of saving many souls and bringing forth much truth, enlightenment, and revelation through teaching the Word of God. Keisha continues to work hard in advocating wholeness, happiness, and well-being for families. Her inspirations are and will continue to include the aid and assistance of women in hopeless situations dealing with addictions, depressions, mental abuse, physical abuse, and emotional abuse. She also continues to mentor and guide other women into their God-given purposes through prayer and serving daily, with the heart of God.

Butterfly Typeface Publishing

"We Make Good Great"

www.butterflytypeface.com

www.ingramcontent.com/pod-product-compliance
Lightning Source LLC
Chambersburg PA
CBHW080249170426
43192CB00014BA/2615